Stock Market Investing for Beginners:

The Easiest Guide to Become
An Investor, Investing for Beginners

Tony Toson

© Copyright 2018 by Tony Toson- All rights reserved.

The following Book is reproduced below with the goal of providing information that is as accurate and reliable as possible. Regardless, purchasing this Book can be seen as consent to the fact that both the publisher and the author of this book are in no way experts on the topics discussed within and that any recommendations or suggestions that are made herein are for entertainment purposes only. Professionals should be consulted as needed prior to undertaking any of the action endorsed herein.

This declaration is deemed fair and valid by both the American Bar Association and the Committee of Publishers Association and is legally binding throughout the United States.

Furthermore, the transmission, duplication, or reproduction of any of the following work including specific information will be considered an illegal act irrespective of if it is done electronically or in print. This extends to creating a secondary or tertiary copy of the work or a recorded copy and is only allowed with the express written consent from the Publisher.

All additional rights reserved.

The information in the following pages is broadly considered a truthful and accurate account of facts and as such, any inattention, use, or misuse of the information in question by the reader will render any resulting actions solely under their purview. There are no scenarios in which the publisher or the original author of this work can be in any fashion deemed liable for any hardship or damages that may befall them after undertaking information described herein.

Additionally, the information in the following pages is intended only for informational purposes and should thus be thought of as universal. As befitting its nature, it is presented without assurance regarding its prolonged validity or interim quality. Trademarks that are mentioned are done without written consent and can in no way be considered an endorsement from the trademark holder.

Table of Contents

Introduction 6

Chapter 1: What Does Every New Investor Need to Know About the Stock Market? 7
- What Is the Stock Market? 9
- How to Invest Money in the Stock Market 10
- Why You Want to Invest in the Stock Market 11
- What You Should Avoid 13

Chapter 2: Will You Need a Stock Broker? 28
- Finding a Stock Broker Through Word of Mouth 31
- What Are the Differences Between a Stock Broker and an Online Stock Broker Firm? 33
- Types of Stock Broker Firms You Can Hire 38
- Where to Find the Best Stock Broker 40
- Shopping for the Perfect Broker 41
- What Should You Expect from a Stock Broker Firm 43
- Which Stock Broker Is Right for You? 45
- What to Avoid with a Stock Broker 49
- Opening an Account with a Broker 52
- Apps That You Can Use to Buy Stock 53
- Apps to Stay Clear Of 62
- What to Look for When Protecting Your Assets 68

Chapter 3: How Much Do You Invest? 87
- When to Buy 88
- How Do You Open a Brokerage Account? 89

How Exactly Does Market Order Help You?..... 94
How Are Stocks Bought and Sold? 99
How Do You Set up a Brokerage Account? 100
Examine Your Account Agreement
Carefully.. 102
Be Patient - Investing Is Not a Race 104
How Much Should You Invest from the
Beginning?.. 104
What Are the Costs of Investing in Stocks,
Bonds, and Mutual Funds? 108
When to Sell.. 112
Charting Your Basics on Buying and Selling.... 113
When Do You Sell Your Stock? 116
Keep an Eye out for the Hands to Move 121
How to Avoid Insider Trading 121
How Is Insider Trading Investigated and
Prosecuted? 123
How Do You Avoid Insider Trading?................124

Chapter 4: Building a Portfolio That You Can
Trust and Create Financial Freedom With 127
GE, General Electric Co. 128
DIS, Walt Disney Co. 128
FB, Facebook 129
AXP, American Express Co. 129
WMT, Wal-Mart Stores..................................... 130
BRK.A/BRK.B, Berkshire Hathaway 130
JNJ, Johnson & Johnson 131
CSCO, Cisco Systems... 131

Conclusion 132

Introduction

The following chapters will discuss everything you need to know to get started with the Stock Market. The details that are laid out in this book are extensive and detail-oriented. You should be able to buy stocks, bonds, and mutual funds with no worries that you are choosing the wrong ones. You should also be able to find the right broker and begin to understand how the fees work and how much money you will need to invest with the minimum investment rates per each Broker.

Chapter 1:
What Does Every New Investor Need to Know About the Stock Market?

The stock market is confusing, to say the least. It can be complicated, exciting, exhilarating, stressful, and financially profitable when done right. So how do you handle the stock market right so that you can gain financial freedom? I would like to say that it is a simple step by step process that everyone can do, but I would be lying. It is not simple, nor is it completely complicated. It is, however, a process that needs complete knowledge and a strategic plan for purchasing and selling your stocks at the right time. So, what exactly are stocks? And how do they benefit you in the long run?

Stocks are shareholder stakes in the company that you purchase them in. For instance, if you purchase stock in Microsoft, you will own a portion of that company at the same amount that is purchased. So, if you purchase stocks that equate to 20% of a company then you have a 20% say so on how the company is run. This gives you a slice of the proverbial pie that is the company and the profitability that this company earns. If you own one or more shares of a company then you become a shareholder. Shareholders will have the advantage of receiving some of the profits or dividends the company receives when it does well. This is determined by the board of directors whether or not the company has performed in a profitable way and has an excess that can be shared with the shareholders.

Shares within the company provide you with several benefits outside of the financial profitability. One of those benefits is the right to have a say so on any and all decisions that will affect the company. This means that when the board holds a meeting and asks for a vote then you are allowed to be a part of that vote. Shares are also called stock or equity.

A share is sold at a set price for the day. The share price is the price with which it can be bought and sold as. This price is determined by the process of supply and demand for each particular company and their products. There are a few factors that determine what the price of the share will be. One of these factors can be that the share has more buyers than there are sellers then the share prices will rise. This means that their shares are in demand, making them a higher commodity. If there are more sellers than there are buyers, then that company's shares will decrease since there are more shares available than there are people to buy them. If the company has a very profitable week then shares within that company become higher to purchase making the company a more valuable asset to have. This means that more people will think that this company makes a great investment for their portfolio. There are also factors that pertain to economics as well as political events that could increase or decrease the share price.

What Is the Stock Market?

The stock market is the machine that drives the sale of stocks and bonds between individuals and companies. The stock market is a business that runs on the buying and selling of stocks. It is a place where an individual is able to see what the stocks or shares within a company are doing, and then purchase the ones that they are interested in or sell the ones that are showing a higher selling price than the purchase price was. The stock market happens within diverse types of marketplaces. Some of them are online and some are in brick and mortar buildings. There are two very well-known exchanges within the US. One of them is the New York Stock Exchange-NYSE, another one is the NASDAQ. There are in fact 14 other locations that are an exchange for stocks or shares. Within the stock market are factors such as the index. This refers to the Dow Jones Industrial Average, which means the measurement of the daily price for 30 of the largest American companies that are sold through the NASDAQ or the New York Stock Exchange. This is a widely used measurement for the condition of the general market as well as the economy within the United States.

How to Invest Money in the Stock Market

In order to invest in the stock market, you will need to start an account with a broker that is reputable. You will also need to have an idea of what amount of money you want to start investing with. It is often thought that you need large sums of money to invest in the stock market; however, this is simply not true. You can actually start to invest in the market with a small bit of money. As little as $50 is a great per month investment budget to start off with. I suggest you start low and build on your investments. Once you get the hang of it you will be able to get a good feel of how to invest, which stocks to buy, when it is the best time to buy, and how much you should invest in. The biggest take away is to develop a healthy habit of putting money into the investments on a regular monthly basis. If you make investing a permanent habit you will be able to have a stronger financial portfolio when you retire.

There are several approaches that can help you start investing in the stock market pretty quickly and gain some financial freedom by the time you are ready to retire.

Why You Want to Invest in the Stock Market

There's a need to have a retirement plan that is versatile and profitable. Everyone is considering what they will do when they get ready to retire. The main concern is how will I take care of my expenses, who will pay my mortgage, and how much money will I need to retire? By investing in the stock market, you can begin to grow your retirement portfolio.

Stocks provide a way to receive the highest potential returns. There is no other investment that will perform better than a stock portfolio. However, stocks do tend to be more volatile than other investment options. Stocks hold value; however, they can drop in value. This drop can decrease their worth. An investment can be minimized by bad luck or simply bad timing, such as when the world went into recession in the 1930s. The price of the stocks can be protracted for a period of time that can last 10 years. That is why you need to take an approach that is a long-term investment.

If you pick stocks that are not good, then you can lose more money over the long term. This creates a pattern of lousy investing decisions. By studying the risks and gaining knowledge about your investments, you can be sure to accept risks that will not be too harmful. Through making proper investments you can begin to create wealth. Investing in the stock market is painless in a sense; however, it does have many rewards. When you invest your money into the stock market you are building a retirement plan, and education plan, as well as a way to enhance your cash flow for recreation. By investing in the stock market, you are leaving financial resources for your family to use after you have passed.

What You Should Avoid

The Stock Market can be a wonderful way to invest your money into companies that will gain you financial freedoms; however, there are a few things that can derail your financial plans. Avoid those possible fatal mistakes that new investors often make, the ones that could ruin your retirement plans.

One key example is the S&P 500 index. What the S&P 500 index means is that there are 500 of the largest companies within the United States market. They are a proxy for the market in and of itself. However, many people will overlook the changes that take place with the S&P. They forget that each year those that own the index will add new companies to the mix and remove some from the mix. For the standard investor, those changes can mean extraordinarily little for them however, some people may experience negative setbacks on their retirement plans. If the person invests in sectors that are narrowly based, this could be an enormous impact. This can be a wake-up call for many people.

Many people who fail at investing are those that do not steadily monitor the market or take a strategic approach to their investments. When the market starts to change, you will need to change out your holding according to the positives and negatives. When the market is shifting, you should update your portfolio. The index gets their combined performance level by the rise and fall of the stock prices for the ones that are mixed in with the index. This number is widely followed by those that are buying and selling stocks. This is then used to obtain a sense of performances by the varied stocks over a specific period to gauge how the stock market is going. Although investing in the S&P can get you a substantial portion of the pot, it does need to be monitored and strategically worked to stay on the up.

Another mistake many investors make is investing at the wrong time. Many people believe that by investing, they should see a return every month. If this is the case, then your alternative investment options are bank CDs. The interest rate within one year is 1% of all deposits. This is prior to inflation and taxes, though. This can make it difficult to reach those retirement goals through this sort of investment, even if you are successfully putting money back. To clearly define your investments as never losing money or always making money, it can derail you prior to ever getting started. So how are you going to define your profitable investments? When are you going to decide that you have reached that point where your profit is at an acceptable point? This means building a future without certainty.

Setting the wrong benchmark can also be something that you should work to avoid when investing in stocks. For instance, you decide that investing in a balanced mutual fund is your best bet. You are concerned that your strategy may not be successful, and by being concerned you compare your performance to the overall performance of the S&P 500 index. You check into your investments and see that it earned 10% even though the overall market only earned 15%. Should you be worried that your mutual fund was not as profitable, or happy that it performed?

Since a mutual fund has a balanced fund this means that it has both a fixed income investment and equity. By investing in the mutual fund, you are taking the least risky approach to invest your money for your portfolio and financial growth in stocks. Because of this, you are not making a fair conclusion for how the performance is affecting your financial growth. As with anything you do there is going to be uncertain goals and growth potential and the stock market is no different.

Uncertainty is a beast and it can get the best of even the most prolific investors. If you have goals of growing your long-term stock portfolio and you plan to do this safely without lots of risks, then you must evaluate the performance over the longer term. You should take a strategy that helps you evaluate the investment approach that you are taking over a period of 15 years. This does not mean that you must invest in the same stock for 15 years. Examine the market and the stocks that you are investing in. Look for evidence that shows their track-record for a long-term period. See how they weathered within the variations in market conditions, and ups and downs.

There are several mistakes many new investors make that can be avoided or managed with strategy and logic. One of these would be to think that the only way to invest in the stock market is to invest in stocks. There are actually several diverse types of stocks as well as bonds, CDs and many other options. One of the stocks that many people ask about is Penny Stocks. Penny Stocks are a completely different investment. The risk is super high and at the same instance, it can be quite profitable when it gives a return. It is best to stay away from penny stocks as well as micro-cap stocks. This can be tricky even for the professionals that have been picking stocks for years. You must know the rules of the stock market and be great at playing the game. The most misunderstood thing about Penny Stocks is that many people believe the stocks that are reported on in news or media can be a great investment. This is so far from the truth; they are not the best stocks to invest in. You may question why the news reports on these Penny Stocks? Simply put, they receive no harm from reporting the advantages of these stocks.

When investing in stocks, you may find that you need to use margin, often times the investor may use too much margin. The margin is the use of borrowed money for purchasing stocks and securities. Margin gives you more options for making extra money; however, it also will exaggerate your loss. This can be a downside. Many investors get carried away with the feeling of having free money; however, the margin is not free money. When you lose with your investments you will end up with a larger debt that obligates you with higher interest rates. This is like buying stocks with your credit card. If you have common sense, then you know that buying stocks with your credit card is a no go. When you use margin excessively you are buying stocks on credit, although the interest rate may be cheaper than the credit card rates are.

When you use margin to invest, you will need to monitor your investments much more strategically since the ups and downs can have small movements within the rate of purchase. If you are not equipped to handle these tasks, then your broker or brokerage firm will need to handle the sale of stocks for the losses you accrued. If you are a new investor you should use margins sparsely. Once you understand the aspects of investing and the dangers then you will be equipped to handle the losses and gains. This will eventually force you to sell off all of your positions when they are at the bottom. This is the point at which you should make a big turnaround.

You also want to monitor who you are taking your advice from. Buying on tips that are unfounded can mean big losses for the investor. Everyone who invests in stocks will eventually make this mistake. However, by not taking the recommendations of your friends and relatives as a sure-fire thing, you can avoid making risky purchases that could mean big losses. Some investment professionals will make unfounded tips as well. These can come from the television or social media outlets that you frequent. You may see a specific stock preached about time and time again and wonder if it is truly a great buy; however, it could simply be the one hit wonder. Since these tips usually do not pan out on the positive side, it is all a speculative gamble.

This does not mean that you will not receive some really terrific tips, just be careful with who you are receiving these tips from. Instead, do your own homework and look into how the stock has been fairing over time. As the famous saying goes; try and try again and with stocks, and you will want to research intensively and extensively. If you are interested in a stock, then that stock should be purchased based on your interest in the company and its products line, not what a broker says about the stock or the media spouts about it. So next time you get your hot tips, check it out before you buy. This will save you in the long run, especially if the stocks go sour. Another way to check into the stock that you got a hot tip on is to get a second opinion from not only investors or an unbiased advisor such as your financial advisor.

Day trading can be profitable; however, many new investors jump into without any experience or previous knowledge about how to functionally do it. Is this something that you are considering? Think twice about participating in day trading. It can become a dangerous cat and mouse game that when done wrong can lead you into financial ruin. It should only be attempted when you have been investing in stocks over a long time period. Day traders may also need to invest in some equipment that is specialized for helping you with your day trading. The average station for day trading can be an investment in and of itself, ranging from $10,000 to $20,000. But the investment that is needed for the day trading can be quite astronomical as well. In order to be a fully functioning day trader with the ability to grow your portfolio, you will need a large amount of money that is available for your trading needs.

Since day trading can happen quickly and needs a faster reaction time, starting day trading with only a few extra thousand in the bank is not as logical as you would think. An online broker does not have a system that is equipped to work as fast as would be needed for a day trader. This can mean a difference between pennies per share and a profitable trade or losing it all together. If you ask a broker how to start successfully day trading, they will tell you to take a course to better understand how to do it effectively.

Consider day trading more intently before investing in the risks of day trading. If you have the expertise and the platform that is necessary for effective success, then day trading can be quite profitable. If you do not handle stress or dealing with risks, then consider investing in a more effective, less stressful way.

If a stock appears cheap, this does not mean that you need to buy it. Not everything cheap is worth purchasing. When investors purchase stocks that are cheap, they are usually basing the price on the 52-week high that the stock has had compared to the current share price. Oftentimes people will gauge that the fallen share has represented a good buy, however, if the company showed a higher share price last year that does not mean that the current year will go up, giving you the hope for a rise again. Instead, it means that you need to analyze the fall in the share price. Find out what has decreased the price of those shares and what factors have taken place over the year. There are many factors that can be taken into account. These can be the deterioration of the fundamentals of the company, a resignation of the CEO, as well as an increasingly competitive factor. These can all factor into the reasons that a stocks price has been lowered. It will also provide you with a clear idea that the stock may not increase anytime soon. This means that for some reason the company can be worth less than it was when the price of the stock had increased. Having a critical eye will help you know why the low share price is not a great buy. It can be a false signal to buy now when you should really gauge what the stock is going to do.

If it looks like a bargain, then it's more than likely is not. Do your research. There is always a reason that is fundamentally strong on why a stock has decreased in price. Do some in-depth research and analyze the investment that you are going to make. Determine if it is really the best investment at this time. Invest in companies that will gain a substantial amount of growth in the future.

Another reason that many first-time investors fail is that they underestimate their ability to be prosperous. Many investors have this complex that inhibits their ability to gain growth in their investments since they believe that only a sophisticated investor is the only one profitable. However, this perception is far from the truth. If you ask a commission-based mutual funds salesman, they will tell you that this is simply not true, however, the majority of them are not profitable themselves. They are underperforming within the broader market. By taking time to do research and learn all you can about investing, you are able to be well-equipped to own a portfolio and make educated investing decisions.

Most of what you need when investing in stocks or mutual funds is to use common sense and some rationality. As an individual investor, you are not liquidly solvent to face the challenges that a larger investment brokerage can, hence, skill is a necessity. As a small investor, having a sound strategy for investing can give you a greater chance of beating the odds and making a sizable profit. Take into account your own abilities and never underestimate it. Do not readily assume that you are unable to perform successfully within the financial market because it is not your day job.

When you overlook the "big picture", you could be missing some really great investments. If you have children, examine what they are playing with and look at the trends. The brands that are most popular can be a valuable resource to research. For instance, who does not know what Coke is? No one, right? The name itself is measuring in the billions of dollar range. Examine what you use in your everyday life and consider what you could not live without. These are the brands that need to be looked into as a major investment potential.

Examine whether or not the company you are investing in is a long-term solution or a fly by night company that will fizz out when the world changes again. For instance, it would be illogical to invest in the typewriter if it is going to be no longer useful in the near future. You should also assess them based on the qualitative standpoint. The Qualitative Analysis is another strategy that is much easier and can be much more effective for differentiating the potential to risk.

The new investor will often compare two companies, and this can lead to conclusions that are completely wrong. Comparisons can help the investor to understand what a better option is when purchasing stocks. It can also designate what to expect with the outcome of the stocks that you are comparing. The amount of consumption for a product can be limited based on the product that you are looking to invest in. For instance, people do not increase their consumption of basic food products but may increase the consumption of internet services or electronics purchases. An average company can perform quite well in the long run. Knowing when to wait it out is necessary for accelerated profit. This means that a company with no market growth is a negative investment.

Investing in wartime can be a tricky subject. We often think that during wartime the world is at a catastrophic loss and wonder will the wheels of commerce keep spinning. If you consider the past and how the market faired during times of war you can begin to see if the market will stand or fall. If in the past it was better to refrain from investing while in war, then it may be a good strategy to avoid the market for a while until you can see an end to the conflict or the fear. As many people are being lost during wartime, the market tends to fair a bit better than you would expect. If you examine the previous war times and how the market faired, you will be able to identify trends and see that the growth was neither lowered nor raised but instead was more consistent. The trends have shown that prior to the actual breaking out of the war, the stock market began to fluctuate, and then once the war actually broke there was a steady market trend that kept the stock market pretty level across the board.

Many investors have seen their portfolio take a turn for the worst and they have allowed this to influence how they feel. They let it put a dent in their pride and take priority over their financial accounts. They held on to investments or bought more shares in that investment even though it was not fairing well. But as a new investor, you need to remember that the operating performance of the company you are investing in will have nothing to do with the price you paid when you purchased your shares. When you see your stocks decrease in the price, you need to examine the reasons behind the decrease and continue your assessment of whether or not they are a great fit for your future investment portfolio. If they are not a great fit for your investment portfolio then do yourself a favor and move the money to a more profitable or better prospect. When you let your pride blind you to make sound investments, you can be making foolish decisions that could cost you more money than you initially invested. Try to be rational with all your decisions and act fast when you find an investment that is not benefiting your portfolio.

Chapter 2:
Will You Need a Stock Broker?

Many new investors ask if they need to invest in a Stock Broker. The answer to this is not so simple. If you know what you are doing, then you can get away with only using an app or online service such as E*trade. However, if you have no clue what you are doing, then you will definitely need an individual Broker to help you through the entire process. One that will walk with you through it and helps you decide which investments are potentially profitable or have the potential to make great gains over time.

If you are planning to invest in the stock market, then you will need to understand the fundamentals of stock market investing first. One of the key things you need to know is that you will need to use a stockbroker no matter what your knowledge of the market is. The stockbroker can be a single person you hire, or it can be done online through a firm like E*Trader. There are huge differences between the two and the online option has only become popular in recent years.

When people started to invest 20 years ago, they would start out by giving Stock Broker money and they would then turn around and invest that money into some stocks while keeping some of it for themselves. The broker would charge fees for their services and make money off the purchases or sales as well as the profits that the individual made from those stocks. Whether you lost money or gained money on the deals that you placed, the Stock Broker would profit either way.

However, this is no longer how it is done. The competition became fiercer and the fees have been reduced, though you may end up with some unexpected fees from the firm that your Broker works with. The cost of investing in Stocks has drastically reduced since the Stock Market and Stock Brokers became an option. Another advantage to investing in stocks came when the online market was developed. This allows you to use a Stock Broker Firm online to invest in stocks. It also allows you to invest with the only fee being the transaction fee for each transaction. You are able to have more control of your portfolio which allows those with more experience in the Stock Market to have a more hands-on approach to their financial planning and purchase of stocks.

I imagine that you are new to the Stock Market and how it can help you with the potential of a financially free future, one that you never thought would be possible. Because you are a new investor, you should hire a Stoke Broker at least for the first few years while you are building your portfolio. A local Stock Broker will be able to help you with a hands-on approach. This will give you someone that you can talk with to help you handle your investments and answer any of the questions that may come up when figuring out the ropes. By building a portfolio with a Broker, you will have a solid foundation to work on for the remainder of your earning years. Hiring a Stock Broker that is local can provide you more protection and help you handle your investments easier; however, it is a bit pricier than the online firms. With anything new in life, you need to go to the source of information, not jump directly into the pool. So, save online Stock Broker Firms for later in your life once you have developed a healthy sense of how to buy or sell, and when the best time for both is. Having a private Stock Broker is not a sign that you are inexperienced, however losing tons of money over and over again is. By buying stock with a less involved Broker, like the online firms, you are placing yourself at risk of losing millions.

Once you gain the experience and expertise that is needed to handle your portfolio on your own then you can jump into the online market and start to use a service like E*Trade. Although E*Trade is not the only online Stock Broker Firm, it is one of the more talked about or popular firms. With the online market, you can begin to choose stocks on your own without the interference of a secondary party, such as a Private Stock Broker. This can be a much cheaper option for you since you will be doing most the work. However, if you choose wrong you will lose millions, so do your homework, research the highs and lows, and never take a hot tip to be a definite win.

Finding a Stock Broker Through Word of Mouth

To find a Stock Broker, it often helps to get referrals from others. Ask around the office, your friend circle, your family and get a few names to do more research on. Talk to those that you were referred to and compile all the data that is needed to make an informed decision. When looking for a Broker, the key is to find a great one. By finding a good broker you should be doing the same amount of research you would for finding a good doctor. Take all the time that is needed to determine if you like them and are able to trust them with your money. When in a close relationship as this one, you will need to have chemistry with the Broker. If you do not find them interesting or trustworthy then you will not be able to work with them.

Many Brokers will solicit business as soon as they meet you. By making it perfectly clear that you are interviewing several Brokers and have not made up your mind on who you will be hiring, this allows you to get an opinion of the Broker based on merit and not on what each one can falsely claim. Do not be worried about asking questions and calling them back with more questions if others present themselves. The answers to the questions you ask should give you a clear idea of what to expect from each one of the Brokers you are interviewing. If you find that the Broker you are asking questions is not capable of taking time out of your day to speak with you, then how can you guarantee that you will have the attention you need when you have turned over your investment accounts to be handled by them.

One of the most important questions that you need to ask of the Broker is how and how much. What am I paying a Broker? And how do I sign up? Brokers will very rarely offer this information to new potential clients.

By choosing a Stock Broker wisely you are able to have a middleman that is in the game for you, not for them. They will be able to celebrate your accomplishments with your investments and feel your losses as well.

What Are the Differences Between a Stock Broker and an Online Stock Broker Firm?

If you only want to invest in some simple CDs and mutual funds, then it would be foolish to hire a Stock Broker since it would cost you too much money in the long run. For CDs and mutual funds, you can do some research and gain some education so that you can invest through an online market. By researching, you will be able to gauge the interest rate of the several types of CDs as well as the reputations of several mutual funds. However, if you want to invest more money in a more volatile or high-stake stock then you should hire a professional Stock Broker. There are some no-frills Brokers that have online accounts, or a full-service brokerage firm will depend on the goals that you have set for your financial portfolio.

An online broker will charge a much smaller fee than the Private Stock Broker does. There is also a fewer hands-on approach that is taken by the online firms. This works well for those that like to be more in control of their stock portfolio. This allows you to pick and choose your mutual funds and stocks by relying on the online firm to process the whole purchase and sale process. The online firm provides background information that is necessary for gaining the knowledge that you need on the products that you are looking at investing in. Prior to making any investments through a specific company, you must ask about trading commissions, other costs, as well as maintenance fees. They may be able to offer additional services to you as well. Sometimes you can receive services such as phone trades, ATM and check writing options, and local offices.

The downside of using a cyber-broker can be that there is an absence of handholding, meaning you are in more control with less face to face question time. You will also be limited to the amount of experienced counsel in instances that the market has turned south. Without that dedicated one on one support, you do not get the human approach to the Stock Market. This means that you can have a much higher risk of difficulties that are technical instead of personal. There are several issues that can arise such as clogged servers, long wait times for customer service, and missing checks.

A full-service broker is a full service for a reason. They tend to offer a large variety of products that are eligible for investing. These include stocks, annuities, bonds, and insurance. They also have counsel sessions that will offer advice as well as research for the beginning investor. The full-service Broker charges higher fees than an online Broker firm would. A full-service Broker is a personal assistant that shops for investments specifically for your financial portfolio.

However, they are paid on a more commission-based payment plan. This means that their income is based on how often you purchase or sell stocks, instead of how well the stocks perform. The Brokers within the firm can be slightly pushy, by offering suggestions for specific transactions that they find as a great investment. They are constantly in the market for new business, so they tend to solicit those that they know or that they see on the street.

A discount Broker will only concentrate on a few product lines at a time. They have a no-frills approach to investing and will not offer advice or research for a new investor. They will often provide an online service that offers to trade through an online Stock Brokerage Firm and charge the investor fewer fees than the full-service Broker would. They are not constantly in a position to solicit for new business which means that they are paid a salary that is not based on your purchases or sells, nor your wins or losses. They make their money through the higher volume of the fees associated with trading. Investors that sign up with these types of Brokers will save a larger sum of money by doing the research that other companies would pay to do for them. They also save money by making their own decisions when it comes to what they are investing in. With a discount broker, you need to be prepared to ask them how and when your orders will be processed since time is crucial. If the trade is delayed, then it could cost the investor more money than is necessary. Also, find out what the discount firm offers for situations when the website is down. If you are interested in a complete overview then you should check AccuInvest.com. This list will compare the direct access brokers and online ones.

Either way, using a Private Stock Broker or an online firm requires you to use a middleman in order to purchase and sell stocks. There is no way around using a Stock Broker of some sort. Every person who is investing in stocks is using a Stock Broker in some way or fashion to allow them the ability to build their portfolio. It just depends on the amount of control you wish to have when investing.

Depending on the knowledge that you have acquired about Stocks and the Stock Market, you may be able to use an online service instead of hiring someone that is about to see you in person and help you through the process. Both options are suitable for several diverse types of people who are investing in the Stock Market. Each one is an ideal solution for creating a financial rich portfolio.

Types of Stock Broker Firms You Can Hire

Full-Service vs. Discount
- There are 60 discount brokerage firms.
- There are more than 60 who provide full-service firms.
- Not every firm is the perfect choice for everyone.

Full-Service Brokers
- Offer a larger variety of products that can grow your financial investment portfolio.
- They offer lots of advice about investments.
- They provide you with the research that you need to hire the best discount broker.
- They offer stocks, derivatives, insurance, annuities, and bonds.
- They charge higher fees.
- Paid mostly by commissions so they

solicit business at all times.

- They are compensated by how often you trade, not by the amount that you earn.
- They are focused on getting you to trade often.

Discount Brokers

- Offer no research or advice.
- They provide no frills when dealing with your transactions.
- They charge lower fees than a full-service firm.
- They offer online order services.
- Paid a fixed salary for each trade they process.
- They do not worry about soliciting new clientele.
- They have a fixed rate of pay that is not based on commissions.
- They make the bulk of their income with a large amount of clientele they sign on.
- They compete based on the reliability of their services and their price.
- The one with the best price gets the

business; they also have the lowest price.

Online trading

- The offer online trading, as do, all other Brokers.
- Have access to your account information when you need it.
- Allows you to trade 24 hours a day.
- Discount brokers will often offer online trading as well as a real person to talk with.
- Real live brokers will cost more when trading as opposed to trading over the internet.

Where to Find the Best Stock Broker

Some of the best stock brokers can be found in the most convenient way, by word of mouth or through some research. Finding a Stock Broker is not a challenging task to do. There are a million and one listings online that can point you in the right direction, however, you want to follow your gut and get all the information that you can about who is going to be handling your money. Be well informed and do not just go with the first person you talk to.

They could end up being the one that either helps you build your financial portfolio through the Stock Market or the one that embezzles money from you.

Shopping for the Perfect Broker

When shopping for a Stock Broker you will need to decide the amount that you are willing to invest in the Stock Market. Decide what you are investing in, such as options, bonds, mutual funds, stocks, and CDs. Do your research to find the best Broker to offer you the best product line and compare the fees that are associated with the services offered. This will include the trading commissions, IRS custodial fees, associated cost to the broker, and account maintenance fees. You can find a guide for all of these with The Missouri Securities Division.

If you log on to MSNBC.com you will be able to find an overview of every full-service broker. There is a securities regulator in every state and they will be able to provide you with a list of properly registered Stock Broker list as well as any complaints that have been raised about those brokers.

There are several online sites that can be used to gain

an advanced knowledge of all of the local brokers and online brokers that are registered and qualified to handle your investment portfolio. By looking on biz.yahoo.com, you can receive a numbered outline that will help you in choosing an online broker. The Motley fool is another site that will provide a comparison chart for brokers that are licensed and working with TD Ameritrade, Power E*Trade, ShareBuilder, and Fidelity. And finally, you can check out the consumersearch.com where you will be able to find a list of the best reviews for online brokers. This will include charts that offer a comparison as well as links.

Next, you need to consider the cost of doing business with the brokers. The typical costs that are assessed by the Stock Brokers can have a range of $7-$20 with those that are discounted, all the way up to $400-$700 for a full-service style firm that provides multiple services to the investors. Some brokerage firms can charge an account maintenance fee of $25-$200 for accounts that invest below the minimum investment required or have a certain number of transactions each year under the minimum requirement. For some small investors, the $160 cost for maintenance can be 8% of their $2,000 stock investment portfolio due to the limited number of trades they perform each year. If you only have a small number of funds to invest, then look into firms that do not have a minimum requirement as well as no maintenance fees. If you are looking for an example of how to calculate your commissions and the difference of cost and profit, then there is a handy downloadable file on the ThinkQuest.org site.

What Should You Expect from a Stock Broker Firm

In order to understand what to expect from a Stock Broker, you first need to understand what a Stock Broker does. To understand what a Broker is doing for your investments, you need to ask someone who operates as a Broker. The role of a Broker can be quite simple:

1. They are a salesperson.
2. They work for a Brokerage Firm.
3. Their job is to carry out the transactions that you place.

To understand better what a broker is and how one operates, let us define the broker's role.

A few of the most frequent questions that Stock Brokers have heard from those that hire them.

- How is a Stock Broker paid?

Brokers are paid by commissions on the sales that are made, by salary if working for a discount broker, and a mix of both when online brokering.

- What is a Stock Brokers qualification?

They are required to pass two licensing exams. These are called Series 7 and 63. Once they successfully complete these, they are allowed to a broker to investors, as well as solicit for business from potential investors, and then purchase stocks on the behalf of the investors.

A Brokerage Firm specializes in the execution of purchases in the Stock Market and in some of the firms they are able to advise on the best possible investments for the investors. Even though they may take on the job of research analysts, they are definitely not one. They may provide an analysis of the stocks that you are examining but they are not fully trained in the analysis of the financial stamina of a company.

Which Stock Broker Is Right for You?

Check into some discount brokers and see if any are right for you. There are several numbers of discount brokers online and in your local community. These are places such as Charles Schwab. They have established a more popular online presence than some of the lesser known companies. They also maintain an advisory or management service that handles your accounts. These discount brokers will provide you with a no-frills website option all the way to a full-service Brokerage Firm. The more you know about the market, the better you can fair at the quick pace that is needed to prosper. However, due to the amount of focus that is needed and the lack of time that you have to react, you will need to have help monitoring your financial portfolio. This person will be able to help you allocate your investment potential. A discount Broker is a great solution for those investors that have stronger opinions about how to spend their money. However, they still need to have a sounding board to bounce ideas off of. They may also like the delicate touch that is given by a personal Broker on occasion.

By obtaining referrals you are able to find one that is trustworthy and gives you the confidence to trust them with your financial goals. It is important to trust the one that is highly involved with your finances. They should be in line with your expectations, and you should have the confidence in the broker you chose and their ability to maintain your investment portfolio, but also review your financial situation, and provide you with a proper assessment of your assets, goals, and income, prior to advising you on your investments.

A full-service firm will be able to help you find someone that can handle some of the other responsibilities that come with complicated personal finances. This can be services such as lawyers. They handle other things that are involved around taxes, as well as estate planning. Prior to hiring a broker, you will need to get a commission schedule for the broker that you are considering. It will give you all the details around the fees that are charged and how much you will pay per transaction. It will also help you know what the broker will be paid by for his services. These are fees that will come out of your sales, trades, and purchases. Check your potential broker's background for any potentially harmful reports. This can be done through the Financial Industry Regulatory Authority website.

Obtain the credentials of all the brokers you are considering before you decide to work with a specific one. Make sure the broker and the firm are qualified and licensed for selling securities. Check the Central Registration Depository for the information that you need to verify their credentials. This information will give you the information that will tell you if the person is licensed within your state and whether or not they have a history of complaints or regulations demerits. You will also be able to learn the broker's education and any job history that they have.

Once you have done all of these steps you can guarantee that you have located the best broker for you. With online brokers or discount brokers, you are only getting what you pay for. If you want no advice, no hand-holding, and no research support then you are fine with one of those services. If you are not prepared to fly it solo then you will need to find a brokerage firm that is more hands-on, and cost slightly higher in fees. This would be a full-service brokerage.

There are several online firms and they are allowing people to purchase stocks online from the comfort of their own homes for a fraction of what it used to cost at the beginning of the Stock Market. Most of the brokers that are able to manage your investment accounts will receive a fixed percentage of the total account. Once your account grows, so do the fees of the investment Brokerage Firm. They will also take an extra fee for steering you to the funds and investments that the firm is able to offer. Some of the brokerage firms will steer the investors to a stock purchase that is on their trading floor only to generate the extra commissions. They will also steer trades or purchases to another firm for extra commissions form that firm. This is perfectly legal in the Stock Brokers job criteria.

Make sure you know exactly where your money is

headed and do not sign any forms at the first meeting or hand any financial statements over either. Meet with a few other candidates and size up the potential brokers before making a full-on decision. A lot of people will glaze over this step and end up with the wrong broker. It is your money and unless you have a ton of money to throw away at a broker that is not prepared to help you properly, then picking the right broker is necessary for your financial security.

What to Avoid with a Stock Broker

There are 3 mistakes that many investors have been making and most of the Stock Brokers will not inform them of these mistakes. This is simply because the broker will profit more by you making these mistakes.

One of these mistakes is as simple as not understanding what a broker's job is. A Stock Broker is considered to be an advisor for finances; however, not all financial advisors are Stock Brokers. There are 3 different versions of financial advisors. They all have distinct roles in your finances and are all licensed differently as well as compensated on a different pay scale. Hiring a Stock Broker can definitely help you, but not hiring one may help you much more. Instead, you may actually want to hire a CPA or another form of specialist which can give you advice on problems that are related to financial situations. This can also save you money and allow you to work with an online brokerage for your investment needs. A Stock Broker actually makes more money by the investor not understanding the role of the different financial advisors. Do not allow yourself to lose a fortune with this simple mistake.

Another thing that you should avoid when picking stocks or a stockbroker is not being aware of when you should avoid taking risks. Brokers love it when you are trading regularly, that is when they make money. They work hard at convincing you to buy stocks so that they can make more commissions. They do not plan on you to know when to sit back and wait on the purchases or trades. They count on the fact that you will trust their every word and trade when they say trade. If you have any short-term financial situations, then holding on to your money is a better option than trading when the risk is high. Do not allow the broker to convince you to buy into an investment that is not right for your financial situation.

And lastly, by not being aware of lower-cost alternative, you are limiting your ability to invest properly. Have all the information on investments such as index funds as well as ETFs; you are able to make better investment choices. If you are the type of investor that buys then holds on to the investment, then you could be killing your own financial portfolio. If you are an investor that is based on performance, then you should be aware that these investments could have a spot in your portfolio sooner or later. A commissioned based Stock Broker can go broke by informing you about these other investments, and they definitely will not encourage you to purchase them.

Although brokers can be difficult to manage, and you definitely need them to be on your side, it is often better to have on then only use an online service. Brokers earn all their commissions because they are trained to be well informed, but they are also trained to not shoot themselves in the pocket. Brokers will provide you with a valuable service that can provide insight into the market, as well as help you be aware of situations that could put your financial portfolio at risk. Sometimes you may find yourself butting heads with your broker, but they are only doing their job. Put your needs first and do research on your own. By taking full control of your portfolio, you will be able to eliminate these complications that could arise when you and the broker butt heads; however, this will also place all the risk in your hands. There are so many disadvantages and advantages that could affect your investments. Weigh the pros versus the cons and consider using both an online market and a personal Stock Broker.

Opening an Account with a Broker

When you decide which route you want to go with your brokerage account, you can begin to place orders. If you have picked your broker, examined all the pros and cons on a specific stock, and determined how much you want to purchase, then you are ready to place an order with the broker that you have chosen.

This is when the hard part begins. What do you do? What type of order will you be able to place? There are only 2 words that you need to learn when purchasing stock, buy and sell. This may sound simple enough, and it really is. There is no need to make it super complicated. You start out by buying a stock that interests you for the long-term and then you sell it because of you either need the money from the sale or you have a feeling that there is somewhere better to place the money.

Later in this book, I will go over this in more detail.

Apps That You Can Use to Buy Stock

The best apps to start trading on are listed below in the order of great to not so great. I hope that this information is able to help you understand a little bit more about how the apps can help you have a more hands-on approach to your stock market investing.

TD Ameritrade App

The best app for trading stocks online is the TD Ameritrade Mobile app. This is one of the largest market firms online and in the country. TD Ameritrade has been offering multiple apps for everyone's needs. They have a basic app that is designed to give you as much power over your investing that you would have on a desktop, only it is housed on an iOS or Android accessible app. It is also available on a windows phone. For someone that is a bit more experienced, you can find that the TD Ameritrade Mobile Trader app is a much more versatile app to use.

If you are a new trader, which I assume you are, since you are here, then the TD Ameritrade Mobile App will offer plenty of options which you will need for your investing strategy. You are able to customize the screens and dashboards for access to research that is optimal for your investing needs. It also allows you to transfer the funds that you need, and obtain market alerts as well as watch videos that will train you in the differences to the types of trades or investments that you can invest in. It will have charts that you can research as well as indicators and analysis that will help you with the decisions that you will need for proper trading.

Robinhood App

The next best option for a proper stock market app would be the Robinhood app. This app launched before the website was ready. This made Robinhood one of the best apps for trading simply because it launched prior to a traditional website. It also provided free stock trades and became one of the best apps available on the market. Robinhood provides options such as stocks and ETFs, but it does not offer investments such as mutual funds. However, it did recently include bitcoin in its supported investments.

The key features of Robinhood are providing you a way to track your stocks as well as keep an eye on the ones that you are watching. You are also able to trade and search for any stock that you are interested in. By entering the trades that you are interested in onto the app, you will be able to own that stock with a simple click. You can do that without any trade fees or commissions paid. If you upgrade to the premium account within the Robinhood platform, you will gain access to margin which allows you to trade more money without the immediate risk. This extends your trading hours as well. Although this is one of the apps with the least amount of options for services, it is the best for free trades.

Acorn App

Next, we jump over to Acorn. Acorn is the best app for those that want to invest but are completely clueless. This makes it the best app for beginners. After linking your bank account, you are able to track and spend money regularly within the app for trading stocks. You can track the regular purchases you spend as well as able to round the change that is left over from a purchase up to a whole dollar amount and use it to invest it in some stocks. If you find you need to invest more money, then you can transfer money from a connected account to the Acorn account and invest manually. Once you have placed dollars into your Acorn account, you are able to automatically start working on your portfolio by purchasing bonds and stocks that are based on the brief Q&A that you completed when you signed into the app. This app will invest exclusively in the ETFs so that you build a diverse portfolio that is broad and in line with your goals for the investments you want to make.

Stash App

Stash is the best one for learners. If you are interested in making investment decisions but you are coming from a level of minimum knowledge and experience with investing, then Stash is a great option for learning and gaining an advantage. Stash gives you the option to start with your investments with a minimum of $5, which will help you with the ability to pick the proper investments while you are gaining knowledge on the investments that you are interested in. Stash also provides articles as well as tips to help the new investor level up their knowledge of the investments they are making while giving them the access to their account that they need for building a portfolio. They place the investments into ETFs, and then these are placed into various investment themes. These themes could be environmental or innovation. By using Stash, you will have a built it coach for your investments.

Stockpile App

If you are looking for an app that is good for kids then Stockpile is your best choice. The stockpile will let you trade stocks like all the other apps. However, this app provides you with the option to gift a single share or a fractional share with super low 99-cents trading fees. Within your own account, you can have fractional trades that allow you to purchase a high-value stock i.e. Google, Apple, Amazon, and such, without paying the $1,000 per share fee. You can use this app to invest in a portion instead of the much lower minimum that is required to invest.

If you are trying to educate your family on stocks, then Stockpile is a way to let you buy and then gift your kids a few shares. This can be a wonderful way to get your kids started in investing. It is also a wonderful way to show teens and families how to build a portfolio by allowing you to include investing in the stock market as a family activity. This gives you an alternative to watching TV as well as teaches your kids about how to manage money and the stock market. By letting kids buy shares or gifting them on gift cards, you can create a portfolio with growth values. Stockpile has several fees that are charged for the use of the platform; however, using it for a one-time gift it is not a bad idea.

When purchasing ETFs on this app you will see fees such as:

- Gift Cards are $2.99.
- A 3% fee is assessed for the value of the gift card.
- A trading fee of $0.99 for using the platform.

For instance, paying $50 for an Apple stock with essential charge, you can add an additional $4.50 which is not too bad if you ask me. One thing to remember is that Stockpile requires an investor to have a social investment number for signing up.

E*TRADE App

With all the big firms out there, you would not believe that E*Trade Mobile would be the 6th option for mobile apps since it once was the pioneer for investing online. E*Trade started online investing options via American Online and Compuserve. This made it a pioneer in the Stock Market online world. They have remained one of the leaders in online trading as well as mobile trading and it still remains at the top of the market for online apps for investing. There are some pretty advanced features that have provided E*Trade with a platform for trading that surpasses most of the others. Once you log on to your E*Trade app, whether in the iOS or Android version, you are able to see the investments that you have made as well as enter some trades for ETFs, stocks, other options, and mutual funds. There are in fact some other complex options for trading. They are also the owners of OptionsHouse which is another option for online trading for stock options, making it a powerful contender as one of the best online apps.

Charles Schwab App

If you are looking for a great stock app as well as a great banking app then Charles Schwab is one of the best. Many Brokers have gotten a wild and crazy hair to open their own investment firm and this is what happened with Charles Schwab. However, none other have done it as good as Schwab. They have provided the best banking and stock trading app to integrate the two into one glorious app that allows you to manage your mobile app and your investment account. Deposit your checks into the app, manage your investments and transfer funds all with the same simple app. Not only is it a great app in the United States but it has a great sister app that works with those that travel internationally. They have the Schwab Investor Checking ATM card that works everywhere with absolutely no fees. Another great advantage to the Schwab app is that it can be used on the Apple, Kindle Fire, and Android devices, which allow you to manage your banking, investments, watch live CNBC, enter some trades, follow your portfolio and the performance, and do copious amounts of research. With Schwab, you are also given the opportunity to pay your bills with the bill pay function. This is housed within the same app that you would buy stocks, mutual funds, ETFs, and other investment options.

TradeHero App

If you are not ready to use real money while investing in the Stock Market, then consider jumping into TradeHero and using fake money to sample the process. This is a Stock Market based game that allows you to experience the Stock Market without having the risk of losing money. They give you $100,000 portfolio to play with on the mobile app or the web platform. This app also allows you to keep track of real stocks that are on the market and their prices with no financial risk. This is a wonderful way to learn how to use the Stock Market to build a portfolio with real-life stocks and prices. You can see the fluctuating prices and how the market can be exciting and profitable. In 2017, this app began to provide a LIVE version that allows you to trade some money that is real as well as virtual currencies. However, you will need to be incredibly careful to ensure that you do not take too much of a risk with real dollars, more so than you meant to within this virtual account. This app does not buy real stock or bonds, but it will use a contract that is derivative to follow the investments in real time, with prices that are accurate. Try sticking with the core trading features within the virtual app.

Now that we have discussed the best of the best in investment apps, the next step is to discuss the ones that you must steer clear of for your own financial safety. As with anything in life, there is a positive and a negative so in the next section I will go over the negatives that could be damaging to your financial freedom in the future.

Apps to Stay Clear Of

As with everything in life, there is going to be a negative to the positive and investment apps are no different. When I listed the best apps to invest with, I did not list any of the negatives to those apps, so I have included that reasoning here. You have to be well informed to know exactly what to expect. I hope that after reading this chapter, you will have enough information to make these decisions without too much trouble.

Acorn App

Acorn may be an amazing app for investing but it has some negative points that I will go over in this section. Many bloggers are preaching about Acorn and this would seem like the app is a great one to use. However, with the knowledge that they are paying $5-$15 per signup to these bloggers that are preaching about their worthiness, you have to wonder if the worthiness of use is warranted. Now you can see how this would be a completely unbiased opinion. Acorn works with your bank to use the change that is left after a purchase within the Acorn app. Acorn will then accumulate the money that they are stashing away, and once they have accrued $5.00, they invest it into a Vanguard ETFs. Acorn then charges $1.00 per every month that you use the app. The problem is that you are able to invest your own money into a Vanguard ETFs free with a Quest Trade or any other institution of finance. On another note, if you are not a frequent spender then you will, unfortunately, have money that is being stashed away in your Acorn account that is not being used and is essentially being wasted. Since Acorn does not allow you to use the money that is stashed in your bank account and you are not able to invest it, your money is losing 1%-2% per year of value for inflation. If you were to stop using Acorn all together and make some regular contributions to the portfolio that you are already beginning to build then you will know exactly how much you have been able to invest, instead of leaving that number up to the crew at Acorn. This also allows you to be able to maximize how hard your money is working for you. If you save yourself $12 per year you will be able to rely on your own investing accouterment instead of this passive investment app.

Betterment App

The next app that I want to point out the negatives is Betterment, which is similar to Wealth Simple. Betterments investment platform has been using its smart, modern brand as a positive to investing with them. Amongst the robo-advisors, the options have become fairly well known and plenty of people are raving about the reviews. But they are simply ignoring the facts. Betterment has a referral program designed to help push the positives among those reviewers. Most the time, a beginning investor is going to get put through the ringer by the management fees that are associated with Betterments costs. Unless you have

$100,000 lying around to invest with no worry of losing it, then you are looking at annual managing fees of at least 0.25% or even greater at 0.35% per year. Betterment does try to provide you with questions that help them to better understand how they can help you build your portfolio, and then they manage it to your recommendations with a tax-smart technology. The only problem is you could accomplish these results most of the time for absolutely free. By simply walking into your bank and opening an investment account.

Banks want customers to open starter investment accounts in order to capture their business, however many find that opening an investment account with an expensive robo-advisor is the way they choose to go. But they are sadly mistaken. It is a much simpler process to walk into the local bank and ask the banker for advice and then open a beginning level style trading account that costs nothing. Many people will think that 0.25% is not a lot of money when considering the MER, or Management Expense Ratio of some of the funds as well as the impact of inflation. That 0.25% is being contributed on top of the present fees that change in the power of purchase within your capital. If you are a brand-new investor, then be absolutely sure that you stay clear of robo-advisor programs such as Betterment and then learn about some DIY skills and strategies that will help.

Robinhood App

Earlier I discussed Robinhood and all the positives that come with using the app but now I want to address the negatives that can take place. Robinhood has a few positive points that make it a great app such as being a commission-free app for investments which has been rising in popularity over the past 2 years. This app is the no-frills trading platform that some people are looking for, or so they say. The trick is that most of the things that make Robinhood great also make it wrong. This app may seem like a great app to use since there are no commissions for each trade, but it is not the ideal app for those that are a novice or inexperienced investors. There are several reasons why this is not the app for new investors, below I will go into detail on why that is.

- New investors are never heavily penalized with commissions. They may pay $10 once or twice after they stuck money in a

Vanguard ETF and then forgot about it. Many would rather invest their money in their financial institution and have access to market research for only $10 a month, instead.

- Robinhood is not in the market of offering mutual funds for trade. ETFs, as well as stocks, can be a great investment; however, a low MER is a better way for a novice investor to get started. By not offering the mutual funds, they are forcing new investors to purchase those mutual funds with their financial institution in a separate investment account along with the ETFs or stock within Robinhood. This can be quite pointless since you can actually purchase all of these stock options with one single account instead of having to separate out the purchases between two accounts.

Next, I will discuss why the experienced investor is not seeing advantages by using the Robinhood app either.

The lack of extensive data can be a major negative for the Robinhood app. Robinhood does not come close to the market research that is offered by other traditional brokers. This will force the investor that is serious about investing to use another source for research if they are using the Robinhood app to do their investing. The mobile app is the only platform that is offered through Robinhood. This can be negative if you are trying to do some day trading.

What to Look for When Protecting Your Assets

When investing in stocks, you need to ask yourself and the broker a few questions in order to protect your assets. Below I have included those questions and the reasons why it is a crucial factor to ask yourself and the broker.

Ask the Broker What the Company Does

You should never buy stock in a company unless you know absolutely what they do to make that money. What does this company make? What are they selling? What service is it that they offer? In what countries are they operating? What is the flagship product that brought them into the market? How much do they sell of this flagship product? Is this company a leader in their field of expertise?

Imagine that this is the first date with someone new. You will need to court this company and find out what makes them special. You would not want to go out with someone who you know nothing about. If you have no idea who the company is then why would you invest in their future? You could potentially be asking for some major troubles if you do invest without enough knowledge.

You should be able to obtain all this information fairly easily. When you use a search engine, you can locate all the information that is needed to learn about the company and what they produce. Read their website and learn what you can about their history and their profit margins. Next, go speak with a family member and inform them of your intention to invest in this company. If they ask you questions, and you can answer all of them without having to relook the company up then you have sufficiently educated yourself enough to purchase stock within that company. Never invest in something you know nothing about.

Price and Earnings Ratio

By understanding what the price and earnings ratio is, you can be better prepared for the fees that it will cost you per dollar. Every broker is different. One broker may charge you $0.40 per every $1.00 earned leaving you with only $0.60 per dollar earned while another one could on charge you $0.20 per dollar earned. Then you have the companies that tout $20 P&E per $1.00. Knowing what the P&E is for the broker that you are working with will help protect your assets in the long run. Just because you hear that a broker has a long history of helping others make lots of money, and another one has a limited amount of experience, does not mean that you need to avoid the one with less experience. It will cost you less to go with the least experienced broker than it would cost to go with the more experienced broker.

This ratio can be easily located by comparing the market price that is current to the cumulative earnings over a period of 4 quarters. Then compare this to similar companies and their P&E. If the company you are working with has a higher P&E than others, then there should be a valid reason. However, if they have a lower P&E, and is growing fast, then this is a company that needs to be watched.

Beta

This is found within the same space as the P&E on the report for all major stocks. The data is provided by companies such as Google, and Yahoo. The Beta will measure the volatility of the company. This means that it measures the moodiness of the companies stock. They measure the moodiness over the past 5 years. You can consider that S&P 500 would be a pillar for mental stability and competency. When the companies that you are purchasing stock in have dropped or rose in value higher than the S&P, and this rise or drop is stretched over the S&P five-year span, it will have a much higher beta. On the beta scale, anything that goes higher than 1 is considered high beta which means elevated risk. This means that anything that is lower than a 1 is considered a minimal risk or low beta. Beta tells us about the risk of cost.

You will need to focus on watching your beta stocks more closely due to these factors. They do have a higher potential to help make you a lot of money, but they also have a higher potential to take more money from you. When a stock has a lower beta, it means that stock is not reacting to the movements of the S&P 500 as it should. This can be known as defensive stock, meaning your money is much safer. You may not make the amount of money you want in the short run, but over time you will prosper. It also means that you can limit your need to watch the stock on a daily basis allowing you to focus on other things.

Dividends

If you are a busy person with the extremely limited amount of time to watch stocks daily, then consider dividends. Dividends are similar to the interest that is accrued within your savings at the bank. You will get a percentage of dividends whether or not the stock price is high. The dividends pay at a rate of 6%, and sometimes more especially in the stocks that the quality is much higher. Prior to purchasing stocks, consider the rate of dividends that it pays out. If you are wishing to place your money in the market and park it there then investing in a stock or stocks that have a higher rate of dividends is the better option.

The Chart

It will take you some time to read the charts, but a basic chart is much easier to grasp. If your stocks chart starts on the lower left hand and ends on the upper right hand, then your stocks are doing great. If the chart is headed in the wrong direction, then you need to steer clear of that stock. Do not try to figure out why the stock is headed down. There are more than enough stocks to choose one that is not failing. If you have strong beliefs in the stock that is failing, then put it on a watch list and watch it over a period of time. See how does it perform and gauge how the company is going to fare within the market. There are many people who believe in investing in stocks that have charts that look scary. This tactic can gain you profit when the companies value increases; however, with the research that they place into it and the time the put into watching these stocks, there is no guarantee that you would be as lucky without the same resources.

The Bottom Line

Nothing can replace the practice of researching the stocks you are interested in until you have exhausted all outlets, and then research some more. A key way to protect the assets that you have is to invest for a long-term and let it ride. Take advantage of your dividend options and locate the stocks that have records that are proven to perform. Unless you have countless man hours to invest in the research and resources that are necessary to utilize the low Beta stocks, finding a stock that is risky and being aggressive with your strategies for trading can and should be avoided at all cost. To minimize any major losses, do not invest unless its failure proof. Invest when and only when you feel confident and have examined all the charts.

Some more factors to look into when examining stocks that you are interested in, and ways to protect your assets, in the long run, can be found below. I have included a few more ways that you should be hyper-vigilant at protecting your asset by examining everything there is to know prior to opening that wallet.

Find out what the price is of the Entire Company that you are considering purchasing from based on the price per share that is being asked at this time. Do your research and make sure that the current price for the shares is not an over exaggerated corporate price for the entire company. The market cap, as some would call the market capitalization, is the cost of the corporation's full acquisition cost. When you add in the debt that the company has acquired then you have the enterprise value. The market cap would be the outstanding shares price for all the common stocks that have been multiplied by the price quoted for each individual share at the given moment. When businesses with 1 million shares that are outstanding have a share price of $75, they would have a market cap that equals $75 million. This calculates with to this by using the equation; 1,000,000x$75 /per=$75,000,000 market cap.

The market cap can be tested to help assess whether someone would be overpaying for the stocks that are purchased. For instance, when eBay and General Motors came onto the internet era, they at one point had the same market cap. In the fiscal year 2000, GM made $3.96 billion in profits and eBay only made $48.3 million, without stock options factoring into the expense. If you had bought stock in either one of them, you would have paid the same exact price per share. You would think that investors would not pay the same price per share for each one of these companies; however, the layman was entranced by the potential of quick profit as well as easy cash options.

Next, you can look at the P&E ratios for stocks. This will provide you with some unbelievably valuable standards to compare for the investment in alternative opportunities.

Another thing to examine is whether or not the company is in the process of buying back their own stocks, thus reducing the outstanding number of shares that count towards their regular over time. Consider that the overall growth of the corporation is not so important when considering the growth per-share. The company that you are considering purchasing shares could be making the same profit and their sales and revenue could be equal for a five-year term. However, this will create returns that could be substantial for the investors. This is only possible because they have lowered the number of total shares that are outstanding.

To simplify this for a layman, think of the investing process like a pizza that is divided into slices. Each slice represents one piece of the pie or share. Would you, as an investor, like a pizza cut into 12 slices or 8? The pizza with 8 slices cut into it is going to have larger pieces of the pie with better options than the one with 12 slices. There will also be fewer people getting a piece of the pie than there would be if you could divide the pie by 12 people. This is basically how the business principles work. When a shareholder reduces the number of pieces of the pie for the company's shares they are then increasing the shareholder's value per share by that much more. If the company's shares are cut into smaller pieces, you as the investor will receive greater benefits and profitability. You also retain a higher ownership ratio. Unfortunately, many of the managing teams are focusing too much on domain building options instead of increasing the bottom line and wealth of the investors that are shareholders.

Consider why you are investing in this particular company. What it is it about this company that makes you want to invest? Do not invest in a company simply because you fell in love with the corporation. Do not invest in a company just because you strongly feel a connection to the products or the people who run it. Consider that the best company in the world could be the one that you invest heavily in and lose out by paying way too much for the shares. The only reasons that you should be investing in a company are that you have examined the fundamentals of the company. Check into the profits, if they have good management, is there a current price too high, examine all the variables by researching the annual reports, 10Q, and the 10K. If you are investing in this company based on any other information, then you are using emotions to control your investing, and this can lead to a speculative guess rather than an actual intelligent strategy for investing. You need to step away from your feelings and leave them out of the equation that you use to select investments with. Use the data that is stone cold facts. This will be more tedious and requires you to be more patient with your investing. You will need to have a willingness to not buy into a company that does not appear to be in the right value market or looks to be undervalued.

Next, you need to consider that when you buy stocks you must be in it for the long run. Are you willing to invest 10-25 plus years in this stock? Are you willing to be patient and let it grow while you grow? If you cannot fully invest in a stock that you can buy and forget about it for 10-20 years, then you need to reconsider your strategy. You should not feel the need to jump from a stock in less than 5 years. If this is the case, then you do not need to own these stocks. When the big guns on Wall Street are attempting to beat the Dow Jones every day, they are setting themselves up for failure. There is a small percentage that will actually succeed at this, but odds are not in your favor. The Dow Jones is a collection of 30 mostly unmanaged stocks. The reality is that portfolios managed by professional brokers are struggling to compete and beat the unmanaged portfolio of long-term holders. This may sound ridiculous, but it is true since the incentive structure of the investors is created by themselves. They are rewarding frenetic activities as well as the strategy names that are flashy. When a portfolio manager attempts to act rationally, they will have a more tough time to attract the assets that they need.

So, how do you reach success? You must select an excellent company that will handle your stocks efficiently, cost you the least amount of money possible for the initial trade, allow you to use a cost dollar average style program, and continue to reinvest your dividends allowing them to sit for a decade to several decades. Just because you know all this does not guarantee there will be only winning stocks, however, it gives you a higher chance of picking them properly. With the long-game, you will be able to take your time and patiently consider the ones that will make a bigger difference to your financial portfolio. This will make you a more competent investor and allow you to gain the knowledge you need to succeed.

Next, I will address the questions that need to be considered when purchasing stock and how to assess whether or not your asset will be healthy or at a loss. One of the most important things about investing is to know all the details before you crack open that wallet and start putting money into stocks. You definitely need to know who you are dealing with as well as what you are supporting.

What is the company's main product line? If you do not understand what they are manufacturing or selling, why would you invest in it? Warren Buffett is one of the greatest investors of his time. Over the past 60 years, he has invested to the tune of millions of dollars. He is famous for only investing in stocks and companies that he fully understands what they do. What does this company produce, do, or sell? Check out their website and gain knowledge about the company that you are considering placing your faith and money into.

Look for these questions when examining the website:

1. Is this company creating a profitable product or service?
2. What are the earnings that have been reported over history and what is the company's outlook for the next 5 years?
3. How much value is placed in this company's stock values?
4. Who are they competing against for sales?
5. Who are the commanding officers of this company?
6. Are their balance sheets clean?
7. Have you examined the companies 10K and 10Q reports?
8. Are there any red flags that need to be examined about their integrity?
9. Are they sustainable in a competitive way?

Can you find evidence on the quarterly and annual reports that would present a red flag about their profitability? Is the company earning a substantial profit or are they just scraping by? What is the net income of this company? Consider the dollar amounts and the share earnings. By doing a quick examination of the older news reports on this company and their past quarterlies, you will have answers that should help you determine if they are on good standing with earnings. Do they have a solid history of earning? Are the companies seeing volatile earnings? If the company is an up and coming Tech Company, do they have the potential to sustain the growth that they will face during the early years? Are they a growing company? When you find a company that is growing at an exponential rate, it can be a wonderful thing. However, on the opposite side of the coin, there is a value that the market is paying for the growth that the company is experiencing as well as the growth that is expected for the future.

There are several ways that can be used to determine the company's value, as well as the price for each earning, and price for every sale. The numbers that you need are easily accessible online at the Streets stock quote page listed under the Key Stabs tab. The P&E is not the perfect way to gauge the earnings, but as investors grow along with their investments, they need more and more information for consideration on price per share when paying for the stock. Another thing to consider is the competition of the company which you are looking to invest in. Do these competitors make more and where do they stack up? Are they one of the biggest in the market for shares within that specific industry? Or is it one of the smallest? Is it in a growing niche that has competitive players within the industry? Is this industry dominated by one single company or several fragmented companies, with the largest one holding only 10% of the business? Investors should always pay close attention to the competition in the foreign market. Foreign markets have a lower cost ratio than the competition and they will be able to put pressure on the margin of profit.

When investing in a company, you will need to examine how clean the company's balance sheets look. A long-term investor who is serious about their investors will need to be able to check the company's balance sheets and see how well the company is reporting. Determine if this company is saddled with a large amount of debt when compared with the earnings. Checking out the earning structure of the company does not give enough information about the companies borrowed money that helped them reach those earnings. You should also examine how much this company spends on research as well as the development of the product. Then examine the inventory levels and how large they are. If they have increased their inventory levels, research, and development, then it is more than likely that the company's sales have dropped.

While examining the website check out who is the managing director of the company. See who is running the show. An individual investor cannot just drop by the company headquarters to introduce themselves to the managing directors, but they can check out the website and see what they can learn about them. If the company is worth investing in, then their website should show you a breakdown of who is on the board or who the CEOs are. This information should include how long that person has been managing this company, as well as the background that qualifies them for this position and the complete history of the company broken down into a small excerpt.

If there is a rotating door of employees and executive employees, then you may want to reconsider investing. Many companies that have a revolving door means that the moral of the company is low and the company may be facing some corporate changes which are affecting the bottom line. As an investor, researching who you are going into business with can be extremely helpful when protecting your assets. The executives are making the big decisions about the company and if they are unstable, then the company is not prosperous and could be closely monitored or major changes are taking place prior to investing in it. You can use several trade publications to dig into the background and history of any company or executive that is managing a company. By reading the companies 10K or 10Q, you can begin to get a bigger picture of the company's annual report. This is what the Securities and Exchange Commission uses to determine the profitability of the company. It is a more in-depth report that is required by every company who is on the Stock Market to file yearly. The 10Q pertains to the quarters within the year and the 10K is the report that compiles the information that is needed at the end of the year. Within the 10Q and 10K, you will be able to see anything that could present a red flag for future or current investors.

This will show the risk that is taken by this company that can be undermining the prospects assets. The companies accounting procedures and operating averages can be a basis to understand the depreciation rates that are affecting the assets and its rate of growth that is assumed by the pensioners. This will give a great bit of insight into whether the company is aggressive enough or too aggressive. Lastly, you will be able to see if the company is sustainable enough. A long-term investor who is series minded will need to know if the companies they are investing in are sustainable.

Chapter 3:
How Much Do You Invest?

Investing in stock can be lucrative but it can also be risky. You may have an increase in profit or a complete wash from your investments. But the first and simplest things you need to consider when buying stocks are the buy order and sell order. This means that you will simply tell the broker exactly how many shares of a specific stock you wish to purchase or sell. Another thing you can do is sell at market for what is called the prevailing market price. You can also sell at the limit which is a certain point at which it is priced or below that price. For instance, placing an order for 100 shares of Amazon stock at a limited price of $140 per share, you are would only be willing to purchase if it is sold at $140 per share or less. When you are selling your stocks, you are allowed to use a stop limit. This is an instruction that allows your broker to sell the shares when they reach below a certain price point. For instance, you have placed a stop limit on the stock you previously purchased. This stop limit is set at $130 and the broker knows that you want these shares to be sold once they fall at or below that price point.

When to Buy

Knowing when to buy a stock is as simple as knowing what you want to buy and also knowing who you are purchasing your stocks through. If you are buying stocks through an online broker, then there are a few steps that you need to take.

First, you need to open your brokerage account. Consider how you wish to trade and find a company that offers lower trade commissions. This can be as little as $7. They should also provide you with some useful tools that you will need to help grow your account.

Secondly, you need to select the stocks that are right for you. Look for a company that has a robust growth in the long run and is a great prospect for your investment portfolio.

Next, you will need to decide the number of shares you wish to buy and at what price you would like to purchase it. Remember that when investing for the first time it is ok for you to start out small.

Lastly, you will need to choose the type of order you will be paying. This can be market or limit for purchases that you will do more often.

How Do You Open a Brokerage Account?

I am sure you, like everyone else in the world, have seen the Stock Market in all its chaotic glory with the clanging of the bell and the yelling of the broker. Although this makes for great entertainment for the mass amount of people who watch movies, it is not in line with reality anymore. In reality, you can hop online and purchase your stocks through an online service for brokers. Opening up a brokerage account is super simple and can be done by the same process of setting up a bank account. You simply log into a brokerage account and complete the application for the account. You then need to provide some sort of proof that you are who you say you are and then fund the account through your bank account. You can also fund the account by transferring funds into the account or mailing in a check to the brokerage firm.

When signing up with a Brokerage firm you should consider a few things:

- How much money do you have to invest? Many of the online Brokers will have minimum investment requirements. This can be as little as $0 all the way to $2,000 plus. The traditional Roth IRA has a minimum of $0 for starting it.

- How often are you planning to trade with this broker? There are many brokerages that are great for beginning investors and most of them have commissions on stock trading that range $5-$10 per trade. A lower commission price can be a crucial factor to those investors who are continually active traders. If you place more than 10 trades per month then this is the way to go. An investor that trades infrequently would need to stay away from the brokers that charge fees for inactivity.

- What amount of support are you

looking for with your stock portfolio? When you consider the difference in one brokerage firm to another, you will find that some offer educational tools, a live human for phone contact, as well as investment guidance, research for stock-trading, email, online chatting, and a branch office that is local. If you need any of these services, then make sure you choose a company that offers these services for you. If not, then go with a less expensive option.

Selecting the stocks that you are interested in investing in is a crucial factor in investing. Once you have signed up for an account and began to fund that account, you will need to look into which stocks you are going to begin adding to your portfolio. A great point to start would be to research companies that you have already had experience with as a consumer. Do not let the real-time market overwhelm you as you are conducting your research. Keep your goals and objectives simple, and look into the companies that you want to invest in and examine whether their business is worthy of investing in. Per Warren Buffet you should invest in a company that you would want to own. And if you know anything about Warren Buffet then you know that he has done well on this philosophy.

Examining the company's annual report will help you with the financial stability of the company. This will give you the narrative of the company and what is happening within their business. It can also provide you with the context for the numbers report. You can examine the SEC filings as well as transcripts, conference calls, analytical tools, quarterly earnings, and up-to-date news. Many of the brokers will provide you with tutorials for using these tools and some even provide a basic conference or seminar for helping you pick your stocks.

Next, you will want to decide on the number of shares that you are willing to invest in. Do not be pressured into buying a certain number of shares to fill your portfolio entirely right away. Start small or ridiculously small and only purchase a single share so that you can get a feel on what it is like to own individual stocks. This will also help you know if you have the stamina to hold out on wanting to trade or ride out the rough times when the stock is going up or down. You will also get the chance to experience minimal losses as well as stress since you did not jump feet first into the market. Sit on that a while, and then consider adding more stock over time so that you can master being a profitable shareholder.

There are several types of orders that can be placed. Determining the order type is important for knowing which one you're purchasing. Below is a cheat sheet to help you know what types there are available.

- Ask - the price the seller is willing to take for the share.
- Bid - the price that the buyers are willing to take for the shares.
- Spread - the difference of the highest bid to the lowest bid.
- Market Order - selling or buying at the best available cost ASAP.
- Limit Order - selling or buying a share at a specified price or better.
- Stop or Stop-Loss Order - the point in which the stock reaches a particular price; the stop price or stop level; and the order is

executed and filled at that price for the entire order.

- Stop-Limit Order - the stop price has reached the trade then turns into a limit order. At which time, it is filled to a point that the specific price has met its limit.

There are a few more moves that can be executed in trades as well as some types of complex orders. You should not bother with these currently, or sometimes never. Many investors are building a great financial portfolio by only using the market order as well as limit order.

How Exactly Does Market Order Help You?

When you use a market order, you are telling the broker and the market that you will accept buys or sells at a price that is the best available option for that market price. This does not apply a price parameter on any of the trades. You are able to execute this immediately and then fill it fully. The only time this does not work is if you are buying millions of shares and then try to do a takeover coup. However, you should not be surprised by the price that is received or given when purchasing a share; it can fluctuate within seconds of the sale or buy. Bid prices or ask prices can be fluid and constantly change throughout your day. This is why you should use a market order when you are purchasing shares of stock that have not experienced wide price swings as well as the steady, large blue-chip stocks instead of the more volatile, smaller companies.

A few factors that are great to know for your investment purchases are listed below:

- A market order is one of the best options to use for buying and hold style investments. These work best when the slight differences in cost can be less important than having to ensure that you have fully executed the trade.
- If you have placed your market order at an after-hours period, then the order will only be placed at the price that is prevailing when the exchange is opened the next day.
- Check with the broker's disclaimer for trade execution. Some of the budget brokers

will bundle customers trades so that they execute all at the same time at the prevailing cost per share. This will be done at the end of the trading day or a specified day or time within that week.

- While a limit order is no guarantee for the actual cost of the order when it executes, there is also no guarantee that this order will be filled either fully, partially or any variation of. These are placed on first to come is first to be served basis, and that can only happen once the market orders were filled, with the stipulation that the stock will stay within a specific set of parameters that allows the time needed for the broker to execute trades.

- Limit orders are actually costing investors more commissions than the market orders. The cost of a limit order is done over a period of one day to several days. If the limit order is being executed in full all at once, it gets a one-day charge. However, if it is executed over several days, they are charged daily till it is fully executed. If the stock has never been able to reach full limits by the time it expires, this trade will not be executed.

If you want more control, then using a limit order is your best option. The limited order allows you to have more control over the cost for the executed trade. When your purchase stock with XYZ and it is trading at $100/share, but you feel $95/share is more in line with the company's value, you will give a limit order to your broker to hold and only execute the purchase order when they meet the asking price of $95/share. If you are selling, a limit order will tell the broker that in order to part ways with those shares the bid must be raised to a specified level that is set by you. Limit orders can be a great tool for the new investor or the expert investor when buying or selling a stock form a smaller company. This can tend to make the experience spread wider and depends fully on the activity of the investor. They tend to be great during the investing periods that can be short-term and volatile, or if the stock price has a more important fulfillment order.

There are of course some more conditions that will place a limit order on a stock to control the length of time the order is able to remain available. This can be all, or none orders that will execute after all the shares that needed to be traded are available at the price point that you set the limit for.

Another one is good for a day order which will only expire after the day has ended for trading. This holds true even when the order is not fulfilled fully. This is good as the canceled order will remain available up until all customers have pulled the plug on the order or it expires out. This can be more than 120 days but no less than 60.

Now, you have a greater understanding of buying and when to buy. You should understand that every broker goes through rough patches where their stocks do not prosper. So, keep your concentration on the end goal, and maintain your perspective on things that are in your control. The market gyrations are nothing that you can control. However, what you can control is:

- Making sure you have acquired the right tools to use for a proper investing portfolio.
- Be ever mindful of the fees that you are being charged. As you get more and more into investing you will find that these fees can significantly decrease your returns.
- Establish a few rules that you will

follow about your investment in order to keep you calm and cool when the other investors would otherwise be panicking.

- If stocks are still scary to you, consider investing in a mutual fund with a broker instead.

How Are Stocks Bought and Sold?

Current issues of stock are sold during an initial public offering. This means that the initial selling of a new issue of stock will take place in a public offering, and they are sold with the prospectus indicating the company's operating procedures. This is then distributed to other parties that are interested in the stock. The investment is brokered by brokers and bankers who are buying up copious amounts of the shares from that specific company and they then divide them into individual sales to their investors. Once the IPO has finished, the shares are then traded at the Stock Market or over the counter.

The stock is mostly purchased through an account with a broker. When you place the buy order, it is handled by the appropriate Stock Market. If the person owning the stock is willing to sell at the suggested price that the buyer wants to pay, then the trade is made. With each trade, a fee or commission is paid to the broker who brokered the deal.

As a stock certificate owner, you are able to transfer the ownership to another person. This makes them an instrument that is negotiable. When you purchase certificates, they are housed within the buyer or brokerages name, on behalf of the investor. If you have a street name registration, then there are several advantages that you obtain if you decide to sell. One of those advantages is that you are not required to sign and then deliver the certificate to the new owner before the sale is completed. You also do not need to worry about any loss of certificates in the event of a sale.

How Do You Set up a Brokerage Account?

Now that you are ready to set up your broker's account, you will need to make 3 decisions that are especially important. The first decision that you must make is the investment decision. The discretionary decision determines the power that is allowed by the broker or agent. Unless told otherwise, the broker or agent can make decisions without your consent. This means they will purchase whatever number of securities of shares they wish to without asking you for the decision process. They also will not consult you about the amounts of time that stocks are available for sale nor the amount that they sell for. Never allow your broker to have discretionary power without seriously thinking of the limitations that it is giving you and the cost that you could incur.

Next, you want to consider how you are paying for the stocks that you purchase. Some people use a cash account which requires the investor to pay for each share they have purchased, in full, when you buy them. A margin will allow you to borrow for investments within the brokerage firm. This can be similar to getting a loan from a loan shark. When you purchase securities, they are held as collateral, and then the interest is charged through the loans.

If the values within the account have fallen lower than a specific number that is required for maintaining the loans, you will be required to pay the balance on the loans down to a more manageable account that is in relation to the new account balance. This can take place in one day or multiple days. This is what most people refer to a margin call. It can require the payments of large sums of money in a potentially limited span of time.

Next, you need to assess the amount of risk that you are able to handle. When you sign up with the brokerage company, you will have to designate the specific investment amount that is your goal in the term of what you are willing to risk. You need to consider choices such as income level, growth ability, as well as an aggressive growth strategy. Consider that you understand the meanings of the terms, and then consider that the level for the risk that you are choosing is at a level that will reflect what you can handle. All investments that you purchase or are recommended by your broker should have a basis in the risk category that is selected.

Examine Your Account Agreement Carefully

You should never sign any legal document without first examining every aspect of it. You should not only examine it but understand it to the fullest of your ability. If you can not fully understand it then ask a lawyer or someone knowledgeable to examine it and explain it to you.

Organize all of your records:

- Signed documents.
- Details that are outlined about your account or investment within the documents.
- Account statements that are periodic.
- Confirmations of transactions.
- Verification that your account errors were corrected in proper documentation.
- Communications with your agent or broker.

Review these documentations as soon as you have them available and then talk about any discrepancies that have been produced by your broker as soon as they're available. Then you will need to follow up with any actionable steps that you should take to be satisfied with the results. Do not allow the broker to send you statements in the mail or confirmation of transactions to another person besides yourself. You will need to verify the accuracy of the accounts that you hold.

Be Patient - Investing Is Not a Race

The investors that have made money quickly are the exception to the rule, so do not consider yourself to be in this exception. There is a long-term commitment to investing in stocks. Make sure you study as much as you need to. Read a ton of books to gain the knowledge that you need to effectively manage your accounts. Attend seminars to learn about all things that pertain to investing. Take any and all professional advice that you can get but do your own research. Once you have obtained the educational level that is needed to be an expert investor, you will have better judgment, a little bit more common sense, and most of all, the patience that you can use to be successful.

How Much Should You Invest from the Beginning?

Should I invest this $1,000 that I have lying around in some stocks? This is a minimum amount that you can use to fund your investments with. But then, as you will soon find, you will be bombarded with minimums for deposits and restrictions, as well as commissions. There is also a need for diversification, especially among a larger amount of other considerations.

So, how do you maximize the return while minimizing the cost?

First, you need to address the amount that is required for the financial institution to open the account. What does this mean? It means that you can not be accepted as a new account unless you have provided a minimum deposit of a certain number of dollars. Depending on the company you are applying with, this sum could be as small as $1,000; however, some of the firms would not allow you to have an open account for less than $10,000.

Stocks

A full-service Stock Broker can provide more services than just simply selling stocks; however, it deals with a higher income clientele. The net worth of their clientele is usually those in the million to billion-dollar annual salary range. The minimum size accounts are sometimes $50,000 and can go even higher for a full-time service broker.

So where does that leave the $1,000 investors at when

they do not have the financial ability to meet that minimum. That leaves them with a discount broker as the only option for investing that hard earned $1,000. A discount broker will have fees that are considerably lower than the ones that you would likely see at the full-service stockbroker. The reason behind the lower fees is that you are in charge of all responsibilities, except the actual broker's job. You will not be able to get the advice that is needed when planning investments. If your investment account only has $1,000, then you are dealing with a minimum deposit issue. There may be a few brokers that will take you on as a client with only a $1,000 minimum, however, some will not even talk with you. You will definitely need to do some homework and shop around.

If you want to go the route of direct purchase, you can directly purchase stocks through sites that allow this type of purchase. However, some of the plans will have minimum requirements for investments. These can range from $100 to $500. When online trading came out, there was a minimum amount of discount brokers who had no minimum restriction deposits. Earlier, I discussed one of the most popular trading sites for these types of trades, ShareBuilder. There are restrictions that you will face as well as higher fees that are assessed for certain trade types. If all you have available for investing is $1,000, then you should start with the ShareBuilder account and consider it as a viable option.

Mutual Funds and Bonds

If you are considering making investments with mutual funds and bonds, then you should be good. The purchase of mutual funds and bonds is a straightforward process with minimum deposit amounts. You can purchase mutual funds and bonds through a brokerage firm, however, they will have the similar deposit rule as they do with stocks. Mutual funds are also able to be purchased with your local bank, and that is often offered at less than $1,000 if you have an already existing relationship with that specific bank.

If you are interested in purchasing any type of government bonds, then you will be able to do this right from a government TreasuryDirect account. When purchasing bonds through this source, you will be faced with a minimum purchasable amount for a bond. This can range from around $1,000 to $100.

What Are the Costs of Investing in Stocks, Bonds, and Mutual Funds?

Commissions are a part of any financial advisors job, and hiring a broker is no different. What you can expect from the cost of the commission fee from your broker can be in a range that will cost you a large amount or a minimum amount. It all depends on the broker and the brokerage firm. Most investment accounts assess a fee every time you purchase a share. The investment amount of $1,000 could eventually be placed in starvation mode when you start to assess the funds and commissions that the broker is charging. If you are expecting to trade often then you will need to understand that the cost can be quite expensive. If you have a minimum investment, then you will see your money draining fast. Every single transaction that you make with your broker will cost you a trading fee. This fee can range from $10 per share trade to $30 per share trade for some of the discount brokers. If you are purchasing one share then you will get only a fee, however, if you are purchasing five different shares then you will have five fees.

If you purchased 5 shares of different companies, with

the $1,000, then you will incur a $50 fee in the cost for trading. This is equivalent to 5% of the $1000. If you tried to invest the full $1,000, then after you have assessed the trading cost your money would be reduced to $950. This is a loss of 5%, prior to the investments ever having a chance to earn anything. Now consider that you decided to sell the stocks that you purchased. You would once again have the same fees assessed. That is a total of $50 that would be assessed again. From the purchase to the sell it would cost you a total of $100, or 10% of the initial amount of the money that you deposited. If those five investments that you purchased and then subsequently sold did not make enough for the fees that it accrued, then you would be at a complete loss by simply playing the Stock Market.

Mutual funds have fees and these can incur from the purchase of. The important thing is that the fees focus on the management expense ratio. This is what is charged by the team that manages the portfolio based on your asset amounts and funds. The higher your MER, the less positive it is for the investor's funds. This is not the end of their fees, though you will also be assessed with sales charges which are generally called loads when you are purchasing mutual funds.

With mutual funds, the fees that are assessed can actually provide you the advantage in relation to the commissions on the stocks. This is because the fees stay the same no matter the amount you invest. So, if you have the minimum amount that is required for investing, then you can open an account and start to invest with minimum amounts of money such as $50 or $100/per in mutual funds. This is called Dollar Cost Average and is a great start at investing.

Diversification can be a risk that you would need to reduce. This is what you would consider a free lunch for investors. If you invest in a larger range of assets, you will be able to lower your risk for one of your investments performing poorly and then severely hurting the whole portfolio. Consider this a bit of financial jargon that expresses "do not put all your eggs into one basket."

Although diversification is something that can be extremely helpful with your financial portfolio, I will discuss it more in the 5th chapter.

Each step you make towards the future is a small amount of money that can eventually bring you a larger financial portfolio. This is more than just selecting the investments that are right. You will, however, need to be aware of the restrictions that are assessed for the investors that are new. Do your homework so that you can locate the minimum requirements that are placed on the deposits and then use that to compare the commissions to that of the brokers. You will not be allowed to be also cost-effective with an individual broker as well as a diversified smaller portion of your expense. Since this is the case, you should consider starting with mutual funds for investing. You must do the research to understand what each investment and strategy will do for you.

Next, let us talk about when you should sell. Selling is a bit trickier than buying since you should be careful about selling too early. But in the next section, I will discuss what you need to look for when trying to sell stock.

When to Sell

There are many programs available to investors to help educate them on stocks and investing. Some of these can be found online at The Motley Fool, American Association of Individual Investors, and several other locations. The best way to locate an educational program on investing is to find out what you need and determine what a good fit for your needs is. By learning when to cut your losses, you can reduce your loss by 7-8%. Even if you are right only a handful of times out of the number of times that you sell your stocks, you should yield a small fortune, even if you were to sell out the stocks quickly.

The hard and fast rule about selling is that you must make sure the market is moving in a direction that is optimal for your portfolio. The absolute rule about selling provides a tool that is critical for all investors and their capital. This is especially important early on in the process of learning. Consider reading material that is geared to help you understand the Stock Market. This can be publications such as IBD's daily, which is a specific break down of the day's action in the market. This publication will keep you clearly informed of the market and its direction through something called a Market Pulse. This will gauge that the market is headed in a confirmed rise or uptrend. This uptrend can also apply some pressure on the correction of the market. When the market is in correction, it means that you are facing a risky period where the market is volatile for placing capital.

Charting Your Basics on Buying and Selling

When you know what to expect, you are able to assess the very basics of stock purchasing which can be as simple as locating the perfect time for purchasing stock. By searching through the IBD Investors Corner periodicals, you are able to follow some basic steps toward your very first properly traded stock:

1. Gauge your earnings as well as the growth in your revenue by learning the basics.
2. Chart pattern bases by learning how to and use them to locate the buy points as well as identify any breakouts.
3. Gain knowledge on when it is best to take your profits and use follow up purchases

to aid you in adding to the position.

4. Gain knowledge on the sell rules that are subtle and identify the rallies that are nearing the peak of the stock for when it is time to acquire the profit.

As you learn to evaluate the basics then you will be able to gain knowledge from the broader CAN SLIM which pertains to trading stratagem. Do not expect this process to be easy nor quick. You will more than likely not become rich in the very first 10-20 trades. However, after the 20th trade, you should see a meaningful change in the confidence level, knowledge base, and skills level that you have obtained using the basics to become an investor that is profitable.

Earlier, we discussed how it is when you start to invest in the Stock Market that you are guaranteed to lose money. I also talked about how it is perfectly okay to lose money especially when you are young and have years to learn. Time will help mitigate the loss so that you can learn how to have profitable investments. Ideally, you do not want it to happen very often. If it is happening to often then you will need to adjust your strategy.

Below is an equation that many new investors will not understand. If asked what they would need to increase their stock back to 100 if it has recently dropped to 50, they will tell you 50, however, they will really need to have an increase of 100 to break even. Why is this? Well, if the stock is at 100 and it drops by 50 then you have lost 50% of the investment. In order to make a profit, you will need to gain 100% to break even because if you only gained 50% you would only be at 75, not 100. This is a lesson that many new investors need to learn prior to dabbling in the Stock Market.

If you think that picking a stock is about picking through charts and graphs then you are definitely destined to lose a large amount of money. If you examine a few different stocks over time, you will see that they have won and lost at different intervals. A company may start out a bit shaky but over time they will increase their profit margin and eventually, if you have stuck around, you can gain more money than you ever expected. For instance, if you purchased Apple stock in the 90s and held on to it through the early 2000s all the way to the current day, you could be looking at a portfolio that is worth millions.

However, if you had sold that stock earlier on in the 90s when the stock crashed a bit then you would have lost out on the best thing that would have ever happened to you.

When Do You Sell Your Stock?

First off, you should consider thinking about buying stock more rather than selling stock. Instead of selling stocks, consider buying stocks as a more lucrative process. Most investors will tell you that out of all the stocks they have invested in, there is only about one or two that have been sold. Buying and holding when investing means that you will win. If your stocks are failing, you will need to have more contexts. Is the general market, overall, falling? Is the competition also facing a loss? If the competition is falling as well, then your stock could be outperforming most of the market. Or if all the other companies are prospering then the failure could be an actual red flag.

There are a few clear-cut moments when it is clearly a clever idea to sell. For instance, imagine that you need a few thousand dollars to purchase a new car. You invest in a stock that is almost, a sure thing, and immediately get a return of $5,000. Once you have made that return, you then sell the stock and cash out. This is a perfectly acceptable way to achieve a short-term goal.

Often times when someone sells stocks in copious quantities they are able to become attractive to someone who is looking for an example of how to handle their stock portfolio. However, this is stupid. When you purchase stocks, you should consider the taxes and fees that come from trading.

If you are sitting in the income bracket of 15 percent:

- You will pay 15% on capital gains tax if you sell under a year.
- You will have to pay 55 taxes on capital gains when you sell beyond a year.

If you are sitting above the 15% bracket for income tax:

- You will pay taxes on the gains for the capital at the rate of income tax level. These can run between 25% and 35% of fees when you sell them in a period under a year.
- You will pay only 15% taxes of capital gains when you have sold in a period of past a year.

The other thing we will have to remember is that people are just horrible at timing the Stock Market. If you see an increase in stocks of up to 10% within this year, you will be able to sell the stock and also keep the 10%, actually a bit less due to taxes or trading fees. If you find that the investment is fundamental and you proceed to hold on to it for a bit of time or longer, then you may infinitely make more than the presumed 10%.

Am I saying to sell it or sit on it? If you are losing money in a stock that is a popular option, then are you really losing? Would you sit on it and let it grow? It is completely possible that by committing to the stock and making a decision that is based on cognitive thinking, you should be able to increase your investment. If you have the patience, you should be able to ride out a worthwhile investment that just took a dive for a bit. However, if not, your options may be a bit more limited. This could mean the difference between investing early and riding out a bad fall. Sometimes a good company is going to be cheap but for the wrong reasons. Consider investing when there is proof of sustainability and only sell when you know that the investment is not going to bounce back.

There are a few surprising statistics that have been analyzed with the S&P, or Standard and Poor's. In 2002, there was a release of this new finding which stated that if during a 10-year period there was a study showing you missed the best days out of that 10-year period; then you would be astonished to learn of the returns that you would lose.

- If you were not trading on the 5 days that were best in that 10-year period, the returns may be dropped by 22.65%.
- If you were not trading on the 10 days that were best, then you will see a return of 37.65%.
- If you happen to have missed 15, 20, and 30 of the best days, of the 10-year period, it will get super worse.

If you are able to identify when those 10 days fall within that 10-year period, then as an investor you have become much smarter than most the other investors in the world. The key here is that you cannot time the market. However, you should not just suffer from the loss in your portfolio, but instead, take a bit of action. A big loss does not mean it is time to sit down and sulk.

- Take some time and do an analysis of your holdings within your portfolio. Determine if they still meet your needs and investment criteria.
- Diversify your investments properly. This will prevent you from being hit hard. Get started with the stocks that you have been meaning to add to your portfolio. This can include international funds. If you want to diversify, add more money into your stocks in a different area or try to shift the focus of your current holding to all new areas.
- Make a list of companies to research for a more diverse portfolio.

There is one key rule for selling: stocks will sell off with a big decline in a single trade-off which makes it hard to sell. This means that in one day a stocks complexion can be completely altered. Consider the way a stock will behave prior to topping off. Certainly, the stock will be orderly and tight with its action. Those with big money will not allow their account to spiral. As I have, I am sure that you have noticed a few big companies who have dropped in price only lightly for a bit of time, and then they head straight back up.

The managers will fund their buying and continue to buy. At this time, the big money will stand around holding out their hands waiting for the less experienced investors to drop their stocks.

Keep an Eye out for the Hands to Move

If you notice that the stocks have decreased in 5, 10, or even 50 points then you will see that the hands will withdraw. If the volume gets torrid then it can get even worse. Just remember that each stock is funded by 80 cents per every dollar that is involved in the trade price.

How to Avoid Insider Trading

Insider trading can mean several things. Below is a break-down of that variety of ways that can show what exactly insider trading is.

> • Purchasing a security for a company that you are a member of. By purchasing stocks or shares for the company that you work for, you could be having insider insight that would not be accessible by the general public. Some of these

people will buy or sell stocks that are based on this information that they obtained from fellow employees expecting a profit when the news of the new feature or product line is released. In the instance that employees are offered stock options, this would be legal, however, if they are purchasing on privately known data that is not public knowledge then it is considered insider trading.

• Doing business with the corporation that you have purchased the stocks on is considered insider trading. This means that bankers, brokers, and lawyers who have access to confidential materials and they use them to purchase stocks in those companies would be insider trading. If they choose to abuse the privilege that they have by being a business partner, they will be purchasing for a quick buck and this is illegal.

• Corporate employees that are friends, and family or acquaintances. If you have a family member that works for the specific company and that family member has insider knowledge, you cannot use that knowledge to purchase stocks for that company with the intent of cashing in once the insider knowledge is active.

- Government officials can also be performing insider trading when they share knowledge and then purchase stocks based on that knowledge. By having access to other corporation's business information, they can be committing insider trading if they use this knowledge to purchase stocks for profit.

- Thieves, corporate spies, and hackers can perform insider trading. These criminals will gain access to corporate information and then use it to conduct fraud of securities.

How Is Insider Trading Investigated and Prosecuted?

The SEC will monitor the sale of stocks to determine if there is any insider trading going on. The market will monitor the securities and track the abnormal patterns of trading. The SEC very rarely gets insider tips on those that are performing insider trading. They usually find it through watching the patterns of specific traders. Once they identify an abnormal pattern, the SEC will pursue the person responsible for it and obtain warrants for their records. Then they will wire-tap their phones and use any means they can to obtain proof. If they obtain enough of the evidence that they need then they will arrest the ones that are guilty and then hand the whole case over to the U.S Attorneys. The attorney will prosecute them to their fullest extent. This is a federal white-collar felony. If sentenced to insider trading, you will face a $5 million dollar fine and can spend up to 20 years in federal prison for each event that was charged with insider trading. Many times, the ones charged with this crime spend much less time in prison.

How Do You Avoid Insider Trading?

Sometimes as a new investor, you can conduct insider trading and not even know that you are doing it. Taking a few precautions can help you to avoid facing these charges. As long as you act with the SEC in mind, you should be able to avoid the risk. Below are a few suggestions to avoid this issue.

1.   Never phrase a question that is asked of a person which could get them to divulge information about a company that is confidential prior to doing a trade. Make sure you do not give them the impression that you want this information. By obtaining insider information, you are just as guilty as the one that trades with the information.

2.   If you receive information from someone you know, verify that it is public knowledge by searching online for it. If you do not find this information anywhere in the media or company website, then you will need to not pursue a trade with that company.

3.   If you hear information that is relevant to one of the companies within your portfolio and you find that it is not open to the public then report it to the SEC. This will be one way that you can prove you do not have intentions of using it for personal gain thus blocking you from being charged with insider trading when the person goes down for it.

4. If you are hearing confidential information, you know this is a breach of confidentiality and moral. If they signed a contract, then they are in breach of their contract. If this is the case, the charge will be much worse. Make sure of the information passed on to you and whether or not it violates the trading statutes.

5. Make sure that the people you work with are clear on what insider trading is and how to avoid the liability. If someone on your team is not informed and presents a situation where the SEC comes in, then you will be liable for the one that was not informed. Make sure your policies are clearly defined. This will block any liability that you have.

6. Be extra careful on how you are repaying favors. You may find yourself in a situation that is insider trading due to someone paying you back for a favor or you are paying them back. Do not offer any confidential information to someone as a favor or payback. This can be called insider trading.

Chapter 4:
Building a Portfolio That You Can Trust and Create Financial Freedom With

New investors will need to shy away from individual ownership of stock. There are several advantages to holding on to individual stocks within the portfolio. These will also include an ability to tailor the portfolio for your values or beliefs. This is to avoid what is called a sin stock. You will have more control over the end cost as well as estate planning and taxes.

If the individual investor is nimble, they can be decisive and quick for their buys and sales. This is different if the mutual fund's manager needs a committee approval on the shift of your portfolio.

So, when considering how to diversify, you should examine these stocks for the advantages that they can have.

By diversifying your portfolio, you are able to obtain more stock options with less of the risk allowing for a better dividend rate. Below I talk about diversified options that will work for you.

GE, General Electric Co.

Making a choice like GE is a strong investment choice. They attract the best of the best and have sustainability for long-term power with earnings. In 2008 and 2009, GE almost brought down the company with a crisis that the company faced. They decided at this time to return to the roots of the industrial platform. In 2015, GE decided to sell many of its valuable assets which increased their sales by $200 billion. If the thing works out for them, GE will have a $90 billion return for the shareholders within dividend and the buyback in 2018.

DIS, Walt Disney Co.

With Disney being a media conglomerate, it has monetized characters that they then went on to franchise across the platforms that they created. These include movies, merchandising, home video, and the Disney parks. While keeping an eye on ESPN, the assets that Disney has with the parks in Shanghai and their Star Wars franchise has helped fuel the growth that is taking place.

FB, Facebook

With Facebook's hyper-vigilant and super-targeted advertising, they are able to market to everyone in some way that is relevant to them. Facebook and Google have dominated the world of online advertising. With WhatsApp, Facebook Messenger, Instagram, and Oculus, this company is positioned with a way to defend its bottom line, and compete with competitors on a stronger ground, allowing for a growth that is continuous.

AXP, American Express Co.

This is a global charge or credit program that is famous for its connection with Warren Buffet. With the 1.6 percent modest dividend rate and a stream of share buybacks that is steady, this company has always been devoted to capital returns for the shareholders. This allows trades to be done at reasonable values.

WMT, Wal-Mart Stores

Wal-Mart's retail and wholesale stores are great investments although not the most exciting one. It performs at a steady rate with a presence that is global. Wal-Mart is a staple in the shopping world as well as the stock market and will not be going anywhere any time soon. Despite the effort of Amazon.com, Wal-Mart will not be leaving the market any time soon. Wal-Mart has invested in e-commerce and this has brought them great rewards. In 2016's 4th quarter, they saw a rise of 36% over the previous year.

BRK.A/BRK.B, Berkshire Hathaway

When investing like the best, you will need to invest in the best of the best, and buying this stock is an effortless way to do this. Warren Buffett purchased this textile building and converted it into a powerful cash flow holding company which is built to last through time. This company is highly insulated from disastrous crashes of the market because it is diversified with a portfolio of businesses that are strong and complimentary. If the market does crash, Berkshire is able to take it in stride by using holders of cash to pick the companies for cheaper. This allows them to have an advantage.

JNJ, Johnson & Johnson

This blue-chip stock is a classic one that should be added to your portfolio. It has been a cornerstone stock for decades, and it is a great option that continues to be conservative for investors that want a stable stock that has strength since they are diversified throughout pharmaceuticals, medical devices, and consumer goods. JNJ is a home for a billion of billion-dollar brands. They have a solid 2.6 dividend percent, which makes it a solid and healthy investment, giving them a decent income for those that sit on the stock.

CSCO, Cisco Systems

This technology giant is a solid stock to buy into for some beginning investors. For the go-to provider of communication, it helps to power the internet. Although Cisco is not a growth business, it is the cash cow that it portrays. Since the P&E ration is below 15, for trading at a modest forward, they can multiple and nearly cut this in half when the price is adjusted for cash which can mean 40% of the entire market.

Conclusion

Thanks for making it through to the end of *Stock Market for Beginners*. I hope this book was informative and able to provide you with all of the tools you will need to achieve your financial goals.

Your next step is to identify and begin the process of defining how much money you would like to start investing with and then sign up with a brokerage firm or an online app. No matter which route you choose, make sure you have done all the research that is needed and you are keeping a close eye on your bottom line. As with any money management situation, do not give full control to someone else. Keep your fingers on the pulse of every transaction and keep your eyes open for anything that may be wrong in your accounting records.

Finally, if you found this book useful in any way, a review on Amazon is always appreciated!